Nordic Christmas Coloring Book for Adults

Nordic Style Xmas Adult Coloring Book, featuring an array of complex and simplistic images.

by The Coloring Book People

ISBN-13: 978-1540594303

ISBN-10: 1540594300

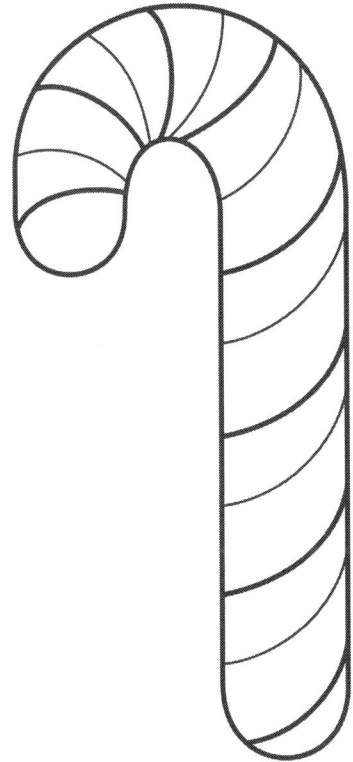

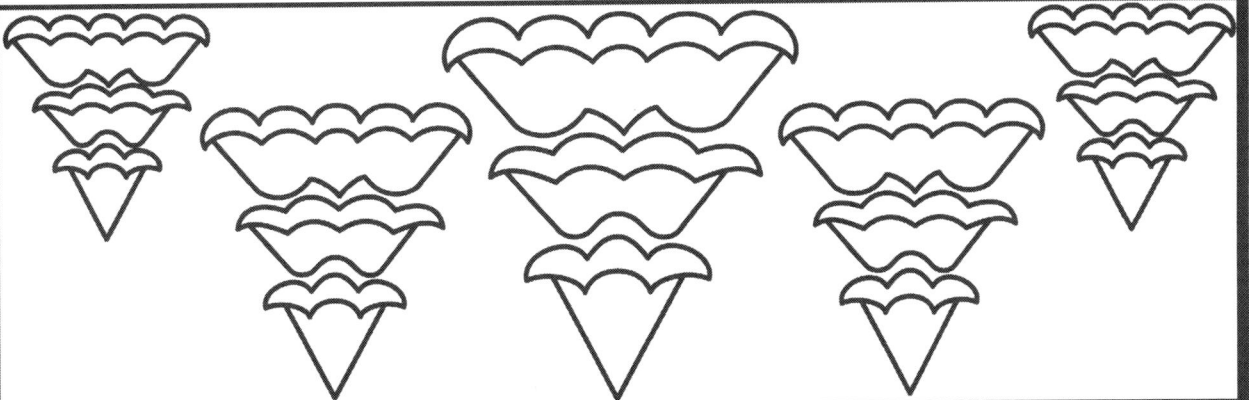

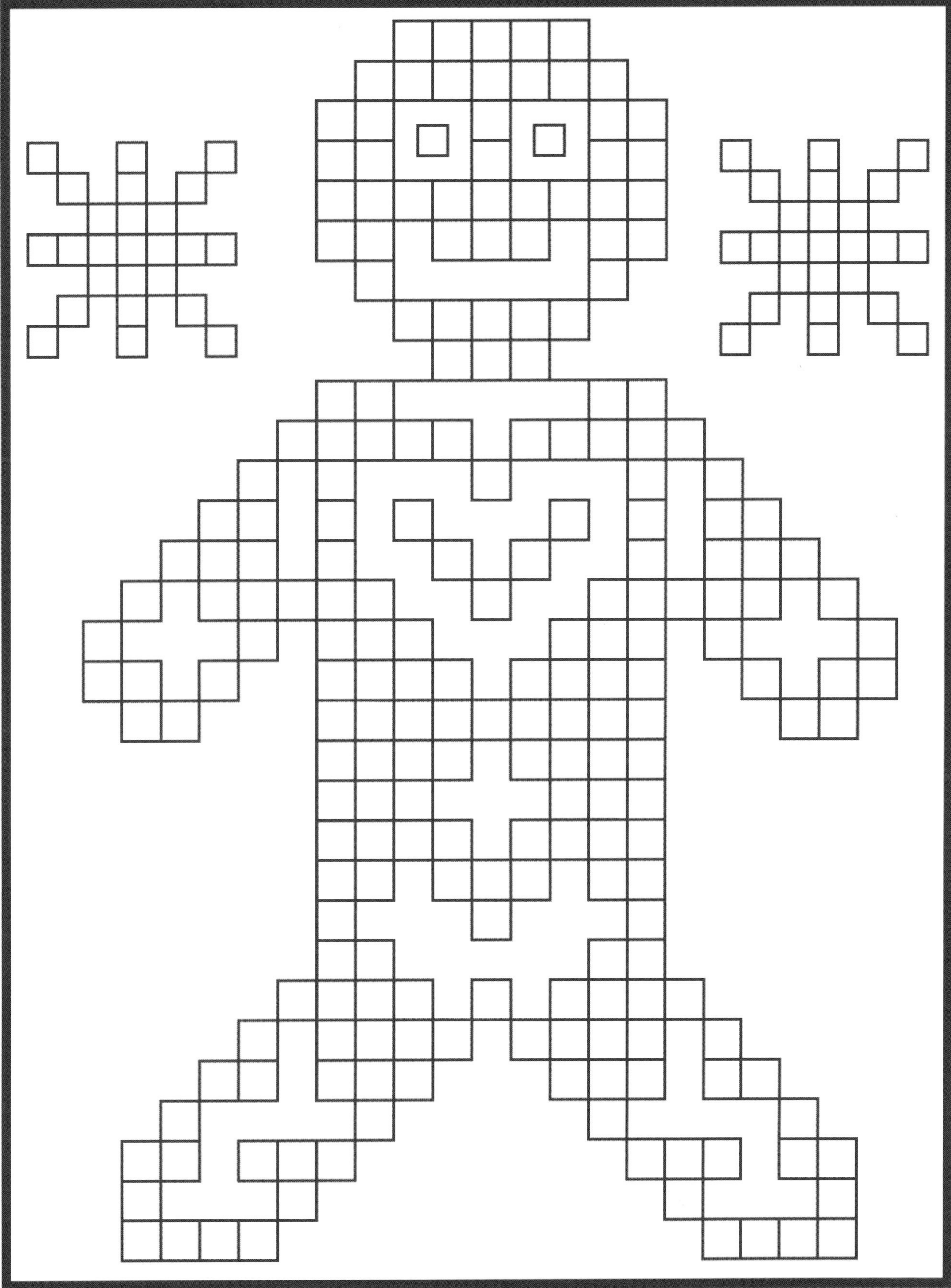

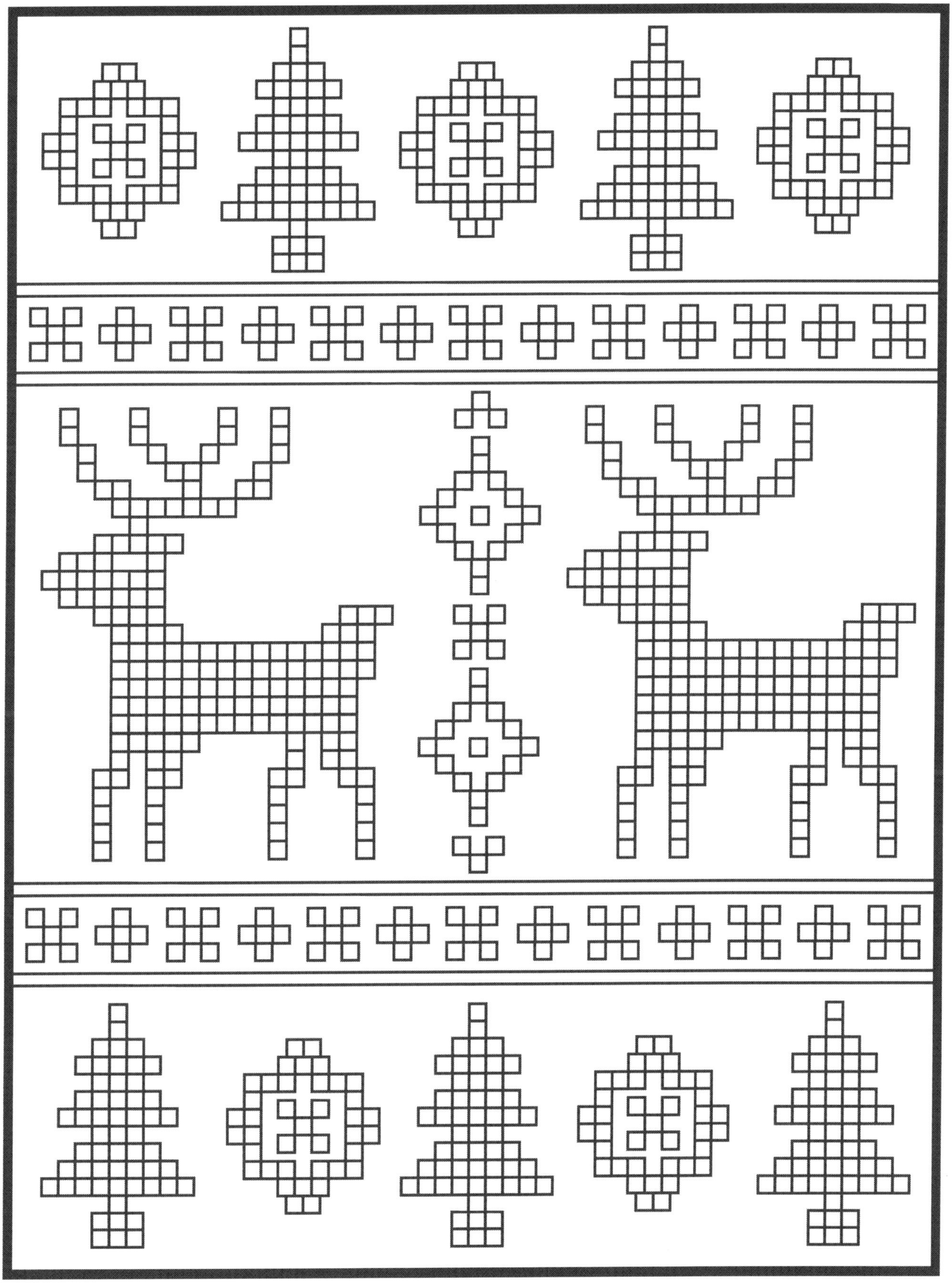

COLOR TEST PAGE

COLOR TEST PAGE